The Night of Electric Bikes

poems by

Josh Feit

Finishing Line Press
Georgetown, Kentucky

The Night of Electric Bikes

*For Rozzy & Jerry
Jefferson High School, Brooklyn
Class of 1951 and 1947*

Copyright © 2023 by Josh Feit
ISBN 979-8-88838-207-3 First Edition
All rights reserved under International and Pan-American Copyright Conventions. No part of this book may be reproduced in any manner whatsoever without written permission from the publisher, except in the case of brief quotations embodied in critical articles and reviews.

ACKNOWLEDGMENTS

The following poems appeared in Feit's first collection, *Shops Close Too Early,* published by Cathexis Northwest Press in 2022: "Encyclopedia of Heresies;" "Linger Factor;" "City Planning Pantoum;" "Dwell Time;" "Athena Dethroned;" "Evelyn McHale Chooses the Tallest Building in the City;" and "Elf Power." Additionally, "The Coronation of Summer" appeared in *Lily Poetry Review;* "Encyclopedia of Heresies" appeared in *CircleShow;* "Obstacle Course" appeared in *Change Seven*; "Linger Factor" appeared in *Vallum*; "In the Course of Life's Events" appeared in *Cathexis Northwest Press*; "City Planning Pantoum" appeared in *High Shelf*; "The Need for Renunciation" appeared in *Vital Sparks*; and "Elf Power" appeared in *Spillway.*

Publisher: Leah Huete de Maines
Editor: Christen Kincaid
Cover Art: Glenn Landberg
Author Photo: Glenn Landberg
Cover Design: Elizabeth Maines McCleavy

Order online: www.finishinglinepress.com
also available on amazon.com

Author inquiries and mail orders:
Finishing Line Press
PO Box 1626
Georgetown, Kentucky 40324
USA

Table of Contents

Isabel Eyeballs 1

Thursday, December 22 2

The Coronation of Summer 3

The Partridge Family Underworld Liberation Front 5

Are They Friends of Your Daughter, Demeter? 6

Catasterism 7

Encyclopedia of Heresies 8

Obstacle Course 9

The Trip to My Parents' House Used to be a Palindrome 10

Linger Factor 12

These Flowers 14

In the Course of Life's Events 15

Wayfinding 17

City Planning Pantoum 18

Dwell Time 19

Athena Dethroned 20

The Need for Renunciation 21

Biking and Woo-woo 22

Dinner 23

Evelyn McHale Chooses the Tallest Building in the City 24

Elf Power 30

The Woman in the Tide Pools Smiles 31

Come In 32

Notes 33

"Smashing the fare boxes at the train stations into wind chimes."
—Eve L. Ewing, "Arrival Day," Electric Arches, 2017

"'The night is a veil, and our Lord ordained the veil!'"
—Naguib Mahfouz, Midaq Alley, 1947

Isabel Eyeballs

how low the wires hang.
She does this daily to determine
if the next tram has any available seats.
She does this for us.

No. No.
Then *Yes,*
this is ours.

Wires at ease
like new friends above

the city.

Thursday, December 22

Work's done, suitcase packed.
No fondness for cars, yet snow
brushed off tenderly.

The Coronation of Summer

I.
There were some tense arguments about dad's driving and Israel
and now the visit seems to be going well.

It's 5:30 on Saturday. I'm making dinner for my elderly mother and father
in my afternoon kitchen Kabbalah.

2 medium jalapeño peppers (cut out the membranes),
1 medium red bell pepper (do the same).

1 yellow onion, and 1 poblano.
Sizzle in a skillet.

With half a teaspoon of black Himalayan salt of the earth,
1 can of refried beans to save the universe.

2 cups of spinach rinsed in the sink.
2 ounces of adobo sauce and turmeric.

Dad is snoozing
Mom is *Becoming Michelle Obama.*

Suddenly, the scene also includes
the upstairs neighbors' apartment with all its noisy interludes.

Have they taken up indoor horseback riding? Living room bowling?
Or maybe a moving company is dragging in crates and tables and a piano?

Luckily, by 6:30, when the enchiladas are served, the clamor has subsided
and lo and behold: We are being serenaded.

Someone is playing a Dvorak sonata. "Do you hear the piano?" I say.
"I do hear something," mom cries. "Is it the traffic on the freeway?"

II.
I'm the oldest person in Bushwick!
The club is a secret handshake up the stairs.
I enjoy processed beats, androgynous computers, and devil's music.

The bartender treats me with love and care
and asks if (at no additional charge) I'd like to add a wheat tincture.
I say yes, dreaming of whiskey tasting like the Sea of Marmara.

He wonders if I get the picture,
and stresses the D in wheat:
"I said," he says, "would you like some weed in that mixture?"

I pass, but when I return to your city, let's plan to meet.

III.
When I'm standing at the sink, she calls me boo.
When I'm drinking this much wine, I'm listening to a family going through
a divorce. When I'm in the airplane bathroom, I'm fainting.
When I'm waking up in an artist's micro-apartment, I'm panicked about texts.
When I'm playing piano in the park, Wendy's Stealing Clothes and I burst out
laughing.
When I'm in a club scrolling through Instagram, I realize Jenny is the same as
Jenny.
I'm in a greenroom,
with a cardboard cutout
of Ruth Bader Ginsburg
when I'm reminiscing.
When I'm putting green sauce on a tamale, I hear it through the grapevine.

When I'm walking to the light rail through an unlit city park with rabbits.

The Partridge Family Underworld Liberation Front

Teeny bopper genius,

narcissus ground to petals of ketamine that time
we snuck out
through windows.

Don't worry, the catastrophe

you're wary of already happened.
When it happened,
life was set in motion, not the reverse.

A catastrophe can be easily confused
with that time the brain didn't match the body,
the lyre didn't match the melody,
and the earth fell from the ground.

Call me Persephone. I stole down
town to Hades' senior recital.
I smuggled in my heart (a tape recorder).
Hypnic jerk scales still telltale.

Teeny bopper
genius, raise your plastic tumbler.

A toast,
that custom when you still believe
you have a chance.

Are They Friends of Your Daughter, Demeter?

> *And the earth, full of roads leading every which way, opened under her*
> —*The Homeric Hymn to Demeter*

I saw the bike lane gods on Pike St.,
with brooms attending
to leaves, decayed pansies and lilies.
Yellow slickers, slung low.
Are they friends of your daughter, Demeter?

I ask because I've never seen municipal workers
looking like this, skills scored
to ancient music, fine raincoats brighter
than any government issue vests.
I saw the bike lane gods on Pike St.

Demeter blamed Persephone's girlfriends for losing track
the very moment before Hades took her daughter below.

Perhaps as punishment,
Demeter tasked them forever-after
with keeping people safe on our slippery planet of roads.

Piles of leaves pose hazards for our 12,000 daily trips,
half of us riding between 7 pm and 1 am;
a plurality at $50,000 below
median income.

When asked what the main purpose of the most recent bike trip was,
43% said riding to hear synths in the park.
Many others said commuting.

Thank you bike lane gods on Pike St.,
your brooms attending to our decayed flowers.

Catasterism

Billie Holiday officially
replaced Athena as the Goddess of Cities
on July 2, 1935
during a recording session
—piano, brass, drum, bass—
at W 57th & Broadway.

Add Jane Jacobs.

Also add Frank O'Hara, who changed
the "Cross of Gold" sermon
into stalactites of light,
record shops, parks, subways.

Add Edward Hopper too. At first glance,

Hopper's canvasses of horizontal cities
seem akin to reminiscence.
But you can't merely glance at Edward Hopper.

Automat, New York Office.

You are drawn in again

to his extents and tentacular fields.

I point you to the subway trains on the ceiling.

Encyclopedia of Heresies

Forty thousand people stopped taking the train.
The next day it was 50,000.
Then 60,000. Then 80,000 people
stopped.

In just a week, an 80% drop
below the baseline before the virus.

It used to be a city

where boyfriends opened
windows at night
to let in cool Sound air.
To let in an Encyclopedia of Heresies.

Like immigration. And
horses galloping in alleys.

But there are no more manifestos
at the Grand St. sandwich shop after shows.

Our blasphemy and bodies are gone.

Our handicrafts,
bridles,
trumpets,
flutes,
jars,
plows,
ships,
and chariots are silent.

Open the window
and what you'll hear is nearness walking away.
The sound of tens of thousands of people
riding an empty train.

Obstacle Course

I inadvertently spilled your coffee today, Mom,
and thought of the time
40 years ago, you set the kitchen on fire.

In the weeks before any father's death,
domestic proofs are dreams in the open,
balanced by everything at hand:
scotch tape holding the liquor cabinet together,
stained carpeting.

In the case of the kitchen fire,
it was your dad who was dying.

You were 50 then, sizzling chicken breasts
in oil; still struggling
to keep kosher.

His rabbinic eyes watching from the living room,
smoke and flames dancing a hora up the wall.

In the case of the spilled coffee, I'm
the one who's 50 now, in the corner,
surrounded by unbalanced end-tables, remotes,
Kleenex, magazines you've subscribed to all my life,

and Dad,

eyes like a kid learning multiplication tables.

I'm trying
to set up his nebulizer.

Mist dancing at his mouth.

The Trip to My Parents' House Used to be a Palindrome

Duffel bag over my shoulder, a 13-minute walk from my apartment to
the train station. Ride the train to the airport stop. Walk to the terminal,
board the plane and fly 3,000 miles. Land. Get off the plane. Walk from the
terminal to the airport stop.
Board and ride to the train station. A 13-minute walk to my parents'
apartment, duffel bag over my shoulder.

For decades, this was the symmetry of visiting
Mom and Dad. A palindrome of trains.

But they've moved.
They are at an assisted living complex now
and the symmetry has been altered.

To see my parents, I must
add a bus ride north
on the #59 to the Transit Center by the Boost Mobile cell phone store.
From there, I cross the highway onto the complex grounds
where the meals smell like Tupperware.

I like the clerk
at the convenience store
where they sell jelly donuts and laundry detergent on site.
The maze of corridors, plastic plants,
and electronic badges is confusing. The meals
taste like Tupperware.

I sneak back across the highway for a whiskey
at a restaurant called Hook & Reel Cajun Seafood.

Is it possible to pretend I'm drinking in a haunt?

It wasn't until a few days later, on the return trip home
that I found symmetry, starting out on the #59
with sleepy passengers on their solemn way.

The bus stops at a red light. Then it turns.
South toward the train station: Voices. It's like
after I water the plants. My apartment turns
into *The Bill Evans Trio: Sunday at The Village Vanguard.*

Linger Factor

The Department of Transportation sidewalk study ranked my neighborhood
15 points above average. A 24% linger factor.

My neighborhood would score even higher
if the DOT surveyed at night
when youth appear in clinamen lines.

The study found this: People who linger are

    talking to other people, or buying   sandwiches,

                              using electronics,
    browsing heirloom tomatoes, playing cello,

    waiting for the bus, watching an opera

singer,   giving directions to other people,   exercising,

  brushing someone's hair away from their face,

stretching in the warm 21st century weather,

showing signs of intoxication such as slurred speech or unfocused eyes,

    doing street upkeep like   gardening or sweeping,

asking   for money or food,

    stopping, to take a cellphone picture of jets descending.

If you believe the local columnist,
these neighborhoods where there's evidence of Dvorak's cello harmonics,
ruin everything.

39% of people who linger are reclining,
sitting on benches, for example, or leaning against a wall.
That's what we were doing.

11% of people lingering are reclining on infrastructure not intended for
reclining, which indicates need for more infrastructure.

I was leaning on a wall talking to you. Waiting for the bus. Eyes unfocused.
Brushing your hair away from your face.
The linger factor was high.

These Flowers

These factory floors are not the only thing here.
There are philodendrons and anemones mixed in to
the landscape making a mockery

of the belief that stop & shops, bus stops,
apartments, and block-long ballrooms
don't belong.

Don't panic, the American composer tells the kids at Lincoln Center.

This one, he says, *is called the Mixolydian Mode, and despite its tongue-twisting name,*
it's perhaps the most appealing mode of all. It's very popular in jazz arrangements.
It has one peculiar note in it. The seventh tone is a half tone lower than the normal one.

He demonstrates, by playing two scales on the piano.

On a summer night, I pretend I'm in a normal family:
My elderly parents wait on the lawn in front of the suburban arts center,
while A Girl Named Count Basie and I run to get the rental car.
I think of us as children bounding off a bus,
running into July's parking lot.

At the hot pot place, all of us make toasts.

As with any arrangement, these flowers
are experts at pretending.

In the Course of Life's Events

I.

On March 23, 2020, the governor issued a proclamation directing all residents, except "Essential Workers," to immediately heed a stay home order.

In addition to grocery workers, canine units, healthcare workers, and weather forecasters; workers at liquor stores that sell food, HVAC engineers; the Defense Industrial Base Sector, and bank employees;

the list of essential workers also included artists.

Artists and musicians providing services through streaming or other technology.

My nieces always talked about their notebooks being filled with words of those who had returned.

II.

Years ago, I found myself sitting across from a bank employee, much younger than me. I wanted to open a checking account.

Disproportionately gleeful, the young man began conducting the interview. Was I planning to buy a house or a car or getting married? He paused. His enthusiasm broken. He straightened his orange tie. I saw he'd scribbled something on my application:

No Life Events.

III.

A couple of weekends into the stay home order, I'd seen two essential artists streaming. Local jazz pianist Marina Albero and local jazz singer Jacqueline Tabor. Their life events are songs.

Instead of saying *piano*, I will say rain. As in: the weather forecast didn't call for rain inside her body and pouring out her fingers. But that's what happened.

Instead of saying *song*, I will say translation. As in: the way the closed captioning transubstantiated Nat King Cole's lyrics, and "be loved" became "believe."

The greatest thing you'll ever learn/Is just to love and believe in return
And that is what happened.

Wayfinding

Greek mythology is about cities not gods.

It's fun to find God,
but I'd rather find that shop with tomato sandwiches.
Extra olive oil, please.

There's also a bike shop.

When you go in

to buy new lights,

the owner asks which kind of light you want:

A light you need to see, or a light you need to be seen.

But never you mind, Apollo. Call my bike Argo.

        Glissando
 across
           the Aurora Bridge.

Who's the sacker of cities now?

City Planning Pantoum

The time it takes your lungs to learn Ravi Shankar's midnight raga is the same as it takes your apartment to turn macadamias into honey. The sweetest story I ever heard was about the boyfriend who greeted his girlfriend at the station platform dressed in her clothes. Their future was doomed. The sidewalk is made of broken verse.

The sweetest story I ever heard was about the girlfriend who hung a hammock of stars beneath the sidewalk canopy for her blind boyfriend. Midnight-to-six is the metric city planners should use to see the sidewalk. The wind is made of apartment buildings. Separatist metrics cannot blur the artless notion that shelter is somehow bad for the neighborhood.

Midnight-to-six is the metric city planners use when they dress in platform shoes to survey the district. A verse from Bo Diddley's *Pretty Thing* is a rendering of Ravi Shankar's evening. The artless notion that additional housing is bad, follows the artless notion that shelter requires mitigation. Apartment buildings are made of our returns from the station.

Greetings, I'm on the art committee for the skate park. The time it takes to turn verses into resources is the same as to dress in silk. The sidewalk is made of stories about boyfriends & girlfriends. Like the one about the future, when midnight asks the canopy: Do your lungs have a favorite song, at this late hour?

Dwell Time

Metro planners are trying to decrease dwell time,
the amount of time the bus or the train, the northbound equinox, waits at
the stop.

There are policy tricks.

All-door boarding,
Off-board payment,
Digital accounts.

There are infrastructure tricks.

Dedicated right of way, queue jumps,
inline stops, so buses don't have to pull in and out of traffic.

And center platforms, so passengers—spies, alcoholics, employees, jesters, extortionists, belly dancers, smooth-skinned lads—can board and exit trains on opposite sides.

We're all trying to reduce the time we spend dwelling.

There are tricks for this too.
Learning Smokey Robinson's three against four.
DMing her mystical final scene.

But, I should tell you—singers, quacks, sorcerers, night walkers—these are only infrastructure fixes.

There are no policy solutions for this condition.

And I should tell her,
if we're smoking pot, we're not sober.

Nor are you Cesar Chavez.
You are 1,871 miles away,
And this app sucks.

Athena Dethroned

Inevitably, a bildungsroman is a story about the city.
This one updates a myth from the 5th century, B.C.
Remember Athena versus Poseidon—a clash
of Immortals at the Acropolis to see who would become the local deity.

Athena knelt and planted a seed and soon
an olive tree was there, a source of sustenance, light,
industry, and rest under its branches.

She became Athena Polias, Goddess of Cities.
For thousands of years, anyway.

Many may not know what the plebeian poets know:
Athena was recently dethroned!

Coming-of-age stories are inevitably
stories about teenagers coming to the city.
At 16, Aldwyn Roberts had a local hit, *Shops Close Too Early*.
He performed it at the district carnival competition and won the top spot—
Calypso King.

He moved to the capital, Port of Spain. He moved to London.
He changed his name to Windrush Generation.

For his clash on Carnaby St.
versus Lady Day and Lady Stardust,
versus Grandmaster Flash and Prince Buster,
versus Frank *unless a subway is handy* O'Hara,

our Calypso King re-wrote *Shops Close Too Early*
as *The Night of Electric Bikes*.

A handy transubstantiation of time into space.

Athena lovingly transferred her title. After all,
aren't the imperatives of youth just the midnights
of middle age: You pedal past houses
and see a piano through a window where fellow insomniacs
gather around its sustenance and light.

The Need for Renunciation

1) The only thing we know about New Lots Ave. is that it's west of here. 2) *All the more reason to go!* 3) To its orchards 4) where fireflies compete with chords. 5) Still, there's a need to renounce it. 6) To arrive in cloth 7) or never go back at all. 8) Please be skeptical 9) of this need. 10) New Lots Ave. is not a parable, 11) it's a place.

Biking and Woo-woo

Three recommendations.

Dry your laundry on a terrace above the black Atlantic.

You can do this in your imagination,
back home on any balcony above
any alley
of alcohol.

Get your eyes checked at the optometrist shop.

Unlike the dentist's or doctor's,
it's the language of happiness.

Take a postprandial stroll.

The theory: it lowers your blood sugar.
The reality: it raises your blood sugar

and your imagination. I make these recommendations
in the fall of the year I met you,
biking and woo-woo
on N Dexter.

Unscientific, yet.
Where I once saw renderings of future cities, I now see
flora as infrastructure.

My clothes the ocean,
my eyes checked.

Dinner

No more salads. Upgrade
to tater tots.

Not as a reactionary show
of machismo,

nor comedy, nor loneliness.

It's an issue of dipping sauce.

That is:
Remember the
applause in the auditorium

after the piano solo.

A chorus of hands.

Evelyn McHale Chooses the Tallest Building in the City

Anhedonic Evelyn McHale lit her WAC uniform on fire.
Her smile looked like a Brooklyn accent.

Her fiancé, Lt. Barry Rhodes, didn't know about pyromancy. So,
when Evelyn burned her bridesmaid's dress after his brother's wedding

—"I never want to see it again," Evelyn said,
as she performed an impromptu exorcism in the basement—

Barry didn't recognize this, nor think anything more
than what he would later tell the newspapers. "She was afraid

she wasn't good enough for me. I thought I talked her out of that,"
he said with his wry Spencer Tracy smile.

Evelyn often told Barry he looked like a young Spencer Tracy,
daydreaming that she herself was Hollywood's Jeanette MacDonald.

They met at a New Year's Eve house party on Long Island.
Barry grew up on the pretty side of Atlantic Ave., a block from the bay.

Now, he was studying on the G.I. bill a few hours west of Manhattan.
Evelyn was as a bookkeeper on Pearl St. in the Financial District.

Evelyn was living at her brother's on the not-pretty side of Atlantic.
There's a photo of her standing in the backyard.

In that picture, as opposed to the famous one,
Evelyn's shoes are on, her eyes are open.

Evelyn McHale was not a nebulous youth
like Bennington art student Paula Weldon,

a vegetarian imagining
the sweet, sharp sensation of being burned alive.

With the exceptions of the exorcism and the WAC fire,
Evelyn wasn't interested in watercolors.

The police report said Paula "disappeared from the face of the earth"
after she "walked into the woods."

That's what Evelyn McHale wanted when she left Barry's abruptly
on May 1, 1947 for the soft train ride of dreams back to the city.

She arrived at Penn Station at 9 am. Instead of continuing on
to work, she went up to the street and walked one block

to the southeast side of 31st and 7th and entered
the brass-tinted lobby of the Hotel Governor Clinton.

The next hour is a mystery.
Did Evelyn find an alcove in the mezzanine,

where a stately settee under starfish chandeliers
became her apse and altar?

Did she summon her childhood medium, a girl she called Margaret
Smith, for morning tea? We don't know.

Which gives us an opportunity to cross the East River,
and go to Queens, to the UN at Flushing Meadow,

where the Egyptian ambassador
has been speaking in riddles.

—"I am prepared not to insist on a vote at this time," Mahmoud Hassan
          Pasha said, but "I will not withdraw my proposal."

                    The General Committee remained
                         bewildered, adjourning

                  at 12:03 in the morning, May 1, 1947.
                  Hassan Pasha was becoming non-aligned.

The UN reconvened at 10 am. With just cause, Hassan Pasha,
reintroduced his proposal.

The termination of the mandate over Palestine. The declaration of
independence.

The UN President said it couldn't be voted on
because it no longer existed.—

The UN is not wholly unrelated to Evelyn McHale.
At that very moment, a UN chauffeur ferried a dignitary to or from

the Empire State Building, and parked the black Cadillac,
pretty as a mausoleum, on W 34th St.

The chauffeur knew a drug store coffee counter
nearby, thereby he was free.

A few blocks southwest, on 31st and 7th Ave.,
Evelyn started her walk into the woods

along the bright mineral sidewalks,
alongside the nervous systems of other people.

Wearing a white scarf and a gray cloth coat,
pearls, gloves, and her favorite shoes, she didn't have far to go.

East on 31st, north on 6th, east on 34th,
into the Art Deco lobby of the Empire State Building.

She purchased a ticket for $3.58, crossed the terrazzo floor
and took the elevator to the observation deck on 86.

She folded her coat over the granite parapet, placed her purse and
makeup kit next to it, and leapt from the tallest building in the world.

Patrolman John Morrissey, working the intersection below,
noticed a white scarf swirling near the upper floors.

Before Morrissey had time to process this,
he heard a crash of glass and staved metal.

Blessed by the wind, Evelyn had
cleared the Empire State Building's geometry.

Unlike the scarf, she fell —122 miles per hour,
20 stories per second—1,050 feet to her death on W 34 St.

She landed like a depth charge into the roof of a UN limousine,
warping its steel frame and shattering its windows.

A young man named Robert Wiles was across the street
with his Graflex camera.

He saw Evelyn, eyes closed and enlightened
in pearls and wreckage, white gloves and bare feet:

Greta Garbo as *The Death of Marat*.
10:44 am, May 1, 1947.

Wiles ran over and snapped a photo of her lifeless body
The Picture of the Week in the next issue of *Life*.

Men in their Midtown hats clotted around the detonated limousine,
in disbelief at the concurrence of violence and grace.

Detective Frank Murray from the W 30th Precinct
raced upstairs and surveyed the 360° brick sky deck.

He saw where Evelyn had neatly left the contents of her life
nestled on the ledge above the city.

The purse contained several dollars,
The makeup compact was stuffed with family photos.

Evelyn's father was a banker. Evelyn's mother left the family
when Evelyn was in high school.

Evelyn had six siblings. They all called Evelyn *Ebby*.
Evelyn Francis McHale was born September 20th, 1923 in Berkeley, CA

to Vincent Richard McHale of St. Louis, MO,
and Helen Constance McHale, née Smith, of Little Rock, AR,

daughter of Margaret Smith, whom Ebby may have tried to contact
in the lobby of the Hotel Governor Clinton.

Vincent got a Wall Street job and settled the family
in a wealthy Westchester suburb along the Hudson North Line

where parties turned out to be slurred hands in the kitchen,
while clusters of strangers sang *Stardust* around the piano.

Evelyn's mother remained upstairs in her mauve bathrobe.
In her hallways. And Ebby wanted to be Jeanette MacDonald.

Impenitent Paula Weldon, wanted
to see the abandoned amusement park by the lake.

Daydreaming she was the Page of Wands,
Paula took the city bus as far as it would go.

In 1940, Vincent and Helen divorced. Vincent got custody
and Evelyn moved with him to St. Louis where she finished

high school. The Normandy High yearbook said, *While quiet,
Evelyn was an intelligent conversationalist on any subject.*

After graduation, Evelyn got a job as an Office Machine Operator
in the Women's Army Corps. When she was discharged,

she burned her uniform, sneaking the blue kerosene can
off base to a copse of willows next to the Mississippi River.

If Lt. Rhodes had walked into the kitchen
five minutes earlier on New Year's Eve 1945 into 1946,

he would have heard Evelyn McHale making claims of divination
to a neighborhood girl home on break from Bennington.

Paula Weldon took the bus past where butchers sell meat,
but didn't find the amusement park.

Detective Murray found the note in Evelyn's pocketbook, scrawled
on butterscotch embossed stationary from the Hotel Governor Clinton.

Tell my father, I have too many of my mother's tendencies.
My fiancé asked me to marry him in June. He is much better off without me.

I don't want anyone in or out of my family to see any part of me.
Could you destroy my body by cremation?

The *New York Times* ran a brief item on pg. 23:
Empire State Leap/Ends Life of Girl, 20.

Evelyn Francis McHale, who leapt from the 86th floor,
was cremated, according to her wish.

The limo driver got the next day off, which,
he complained to his wife, was wholly unnecessary.

Nonetheless, the couple took advantage of the unforeseen
holiday by going for a pleasure drive

along the Queensboro Bridge into Manhattan
with their scarves swirling.

Elf Power

During a 20th century prom,
Megan and I cut out and saw
the Velvet Monkeys at 9:30 Club.

We were
dressed better than anyone there.

On a smart phone in the next century,
A robot asks me where
I left the bike share.

Listen closely robot: Probably outside the pizza place.

The Woman in the Tide Pools Smiles

En route, en route, en route

—although we didn't know it yet—

to the courtyard in the art
museum at the heart
of the state.

The man at the beach asked *how are you doing?*
A loaded question.

We're singing a Prince song, I said.

The woman in the tide pools smiles.
His Labor Party sister?

When we get to the museum,
I count the starfish.

I must keep a list of these imaginary places.

Come In

Clubs are early indicators of what lies beneath Jupiter's
pretty clouds. The first to offer dancing.

Just a few years ago, the first hanging

posters
saying you're safe here. I noticed this standing

in line at the DoNormaal show and thought, *huh, that's cool.*
Come in.

Courtyards rest beneath lindens like clubs are early indicators
of what lies beneath Earth's green clouds.

The Labor government made an early effort,
but after that, it was only dance hall walls shaking with neo-realism,

offering expansion, because they know realism
will falter.

Notes:

"Linger Factor"
Parts of this poem take language from the City of Seattle's Department of Transportation 2018 public life study.

"These Flowers"
The italicized portion quotes Leonard Bernstein from a November 1966 episode of CBS' *Young People's Concert* TV series.

"In the Course of Life's Events"
Portions of this poem are taken from Washington Governor Jay Inslee's official COVID-19 pandemic Stay-Home order issued in late March, 2020. Marina Albero and Jacqueline Tabor are two Seattle-based jazz musicians. The line *"The greatest thing you'll ever learn/Is just to love and believe in return"* quotes a TV closed-caption misquote of Nat King Cole's lyric *"The greatest thing you'll ever learn/Is just to love and be loved in return"* from Cole's 1948 song "Nature Boy."

"Athena Dethroned"
Aldwyn Roberts is the birthname of Lord Kitchener, a 1950s calypso star; the line "unless a subway is handy" is taken from Frank O'Hara's 1957 poem "Meditations in an Emergency."

"Evelyn McHale Chooses the Tallest Building in the City"
The headline to the *New York Times*' May 2, 1947 pg. 23 story about Evelyn McHale's suicide—*"Empire State Leap/Ends Life of Girl, 20,"*—misstated her age. Evelyn McHale was 23.

"Come In"
DoNormaal was Seattle's most exciting hip-hop act circa 2017.

Josh Feit is a longtime Seattle journalist. He co-founded the independent Seattle news site PubliCola, where he reported on public policy for nearly a decade. Prior to that, Feit was the news editor at Seattle's alternative weekly, *The Stranger*. More recently, Feit has worked as a speechwriter; first for the Seattle Mayor's Office and currently for Sound Transit, Seattle's regional transit agency. He continues to write a city planning column for PubliCola.

Feit's poetry has been published in *Spillway, Vallum, the Halcyone Literary Review,* and *CircleShow,* among other journals. His first poetry collection, *Shops Close Too Early,* was published by Cathexis Northwest Press in 2022. He was a finalist for the 2021 Wolfson Chapbook Poetry Prize and the 2019 Lily Poetry Prize. He was shortlisted for the 2020 Vallum Award for Poetry and won Honorable Mention. You can find him online at www.joshfeitpoetry.com. He lives in Seattle's Capitol Hill neighborhood, which has some of the deepest tree canopy in the city, alongside some of Seattle's densest housing. You have it backwards, NIMBYs.

www.ingramcontent.com/pod-product-compliance
Lightning Source LLC
Chambersburg PA
CBHW022123090426
42743CB00008B/984